Chapter 7 features 800+ pages
of printable alphabet materials for use
with the activities in this book.

Download Chapter 7 at:

www.giftofcuriosity.com/chapter7/

Order online: http://www.giftofcuriosity.com/product/101-ways-to-teach-the-alphabet/
Questions and support: katie@giftofcuriosity.com

Terms of Use. You may download, save, and print the Chapter 7 printable alphabet materials for personal and/or classroom use only.

Notice of Liability. This information is offered as a resource. No claims or guarantees regarding the results of doing these activities is expressed or implied.

Note on Safety. Many of the activities in this book use small objects that can be a choking hazard, and as such are not appropriate for children under the age of 3. Adults must use good judgment and appropriate caution to ensure that children engage in the activities and use the materials safely.

ABOUT THE AUTHOR

Katie Stokes received her M.Ed. in Policy, Organization, and Leadership Studies and her Ph.D. in Child Development from Stanford University. In addition, she has more than 20 years of experience working with children from preschool through high school.

Early in her career, Katie was responsible for developing, teaching, and evaluating community-based literacy programs for preschool and early elementary children. As part of this work, she focused on supporting and including parents as active partners in the development of their children's literacy skills.

Katie also dedicated several years to academic research focused on understanding how family practices and community contexts support children's bilingual language and literacy development in English and Spanish. She has published her work in peer-reviewed journals and presented her findings at conferences across the United States.

More recently, Katie founded Gift of Curiosity to share hands-on, developmentally appropriate learning activities with parents, teachers, and caregivers all over the world.

Her *most* important job, however, is partnering with her husband to raise two curious children whom she educates at home.

WHO THIS BOOK IS FOR

This book is for parents, teachers, and caregivers of children ages 2 to 7.

Of course, not all two-year-olds are ready to learn the alphabet, and many seven-year-olds are way past learning the alphabet. But for children in this age range who are ready to learn their letters and who could benefit from some assistance, this book provides caring adults with a wealth of helpful ideas to support children's learning at various stages.

Younger children will most likely begin with simple letter recognition activities, while older children will be ready for learning letter sounds, practicing letter formation, and doing case matching activities. Always follow your child's lead to see what activities they are interested in and ready for.

Please note that many of the activities in this book use materials that are a choking hazard for children under the age of 3. Use good judgment about what materials and activities are safe for your child.

HOW TO USE THIS BOOK

How this book is structured

Chapter 1 explains why teaching the alphabet is so vital to your child's future reading success, and how to teach letters in a way that will maximize your child's learning.

Chapters 2 through 5 are where the fun begins! In these chapters you will find 101 hands-on, multi-sensory alphabet activities, organized into four separate categories:

- Chapter 2: Activities that teach letter recognition
- Chapter 3: Activities that teach letter sounds
- Chapter 4: Activities that teach letter formation
- Chapter 5: Activities that teach letter case matching

Although many of the activities support more than one category of letter knowledge, they have been grouped in this way to make it easier for you to find the right activity for your child at all stages of their letter learning development.

Chapter 6 features useful reference materials. Chapter 7, which you must download separately following the instructions at the beginning of this book, includes printable resources for doing many of the activities referenced in Chapters 2 through 5.

Selecting activities

Use the activities in this book as a *guide*. Pick and choose the activities you think will most appeal to your child. Repeat an activity for as long as your child shows interest. If your child shows no interest, simply put the materials away and try again at a later date.

Feel free to modify the activities to suit your situation. You may substitute materials you have on hand for materials listed in the book.

Finally, letter learning can be *fun* if you keep things light and playful. Be enthusiastic. Don't stress over mistakes. And most importantly, enjoy the process.

USEFUL SUPPLIES

Below is a partial list of supplies that are good to have on hand as part of your alphabet teaching "tool box." The specific supplies needed for each activity are listed on the activity pages in Chapters 2 through 5. Very often, materials you already own can be easily substituted for materials recommended in the book, allowing you to do the activity with your child at no extra expense.

For a complete list of supplies and for ideas on where to purchase them, visit http://www.giftofcuriosity.com/101-ways-to-teach-the-alphabet-materials-list/

Alphabet supplies

- Montessori moveable alphabet
- Montessori sandpaper letters
- Alphabet puzzle
- Alphabet stamps
- Letter beads
- Letter tiles (e.g., such as those from *Bananagrams* or *Scrabble*)

Art supplies

- Coloring supplies (e.g., crayons, markers)
- Pencils
- Dot markers
- Sidewalk chalk
- Tempera paints
- Watercolor paints
- Paint brushes
- Child-friendly scissors
- Scissors (for adults)
- Paper cutter

Printing supplies

- Printer
- Printer paper
- Cardstock (printer-size)
- Laminator

White board supplies

- White board
- Dry erase markers
- White board eraser

Other useful supplies

- Dot stickers 1 inch (2.5 cm) in diameter
- Sticky notes
- Dice
- Painter's tape
- Pocket cubes
- Small items to use as place markers (e.g., glass gems, small rocks, coins)

TABLE OF CONTENTS

Chapter 4
Activities That Teach Letter Formation...................... 80

Chapter 5
Activities That Teach Letter Case Matching 116

Chapter 6
Reference Resources 130

Chapter 7
Printable Resources... **135**

Download Chapter 7 at:
www.giftofcuriosity.com/chapter7/

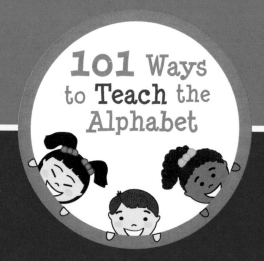

101 Ways
to **Teach** the
Alphabet

CHAPTER ONE

· ·

Why Teach
the Alphabet?

Why is teaching the alphabet so important?

How do children learn to read? And what pre-reading skills help them learn to read easily?

A great deal of educational research has been devoted to answering these questions. One important finding to emerge from the research is that there is a very strong relationship between knowing the alphabet and becoming a successful reader.[1,3,14]

In the 1960s, researchers Guy Bond and Robert Dykstra assessed children on a number of literacy skills and then measured their growth in reading skills over time. They shared their findings in a groundbreaking report on first grade reading development and instruction.[2] Of all the literacy skills they initially measured, children's letter knowledge proved to be the strongest predictor of first year reading achievement.

Subsequent research has confirmed that the ability to identify the letters of the alphabet is strongly associated with reading skills through third grade, and continues to be an important predictor of reading achievement through at least seventh grade.[1,7,10,15]

The implications of this research are clear: **Teaching the alphabet is one of the most important tasks adults can engage in to prepare children for success in reading.**

How does alphabet knowledge support reading?

Alphabet knowledge supports the development of reading skills in at least three ways.[1]

First, when children can recognize letters quickly and accurately, they free up cognitive resources to attend to other tasks of reading, such as sounding out words and comprehending text.

Second, a letter's name often provides a clue about the sounds it makes.[7] Many letters include the letter sound at either the beginning of the letter's name (e.g., 'J' and 'T') or the end of the letter's name (e.g., 'M' and 'S'). Instructional approaches that teach letter names

along with letter sounds are more effective at helping children learn letter sounds than approaches that teach letter sounds alone.[13]

Finally, teaching letter names gives children a common language to discuss letters, which is important because many letters make more than one sound (e.g., 'A' makes both the /ă/ and /ā/ sounds), and many sounds are produced by more than one letter (e.g., the /j/ sound is made by both 'J' and 'G'). Furthermore, letter names provide a connection between uppercase and lowercase letters, as children must learn that 'A' and 'a' are two versions of the same letter.

What does it mean to "know the alphabet?"

When we say that a child "knows the alphabet," we mean that a child has acquired knowledge and skills in four distinct areas. These include knowledge of letter shapes, knowledge of letter names, knowledge of letter sounds, and the ability to write letters.[12]

Letter shape knowledge

To learn letter shapes, children must pay attention to key visual features such as the letter's shape, orientation, and directionality.[16] Children must also learn to recognize letters even when presented in a variety of sizes, fonts, handwriting styles, and cases.[8]

Letter name knowledge

Learning letter names requires understanding that letters are symbols, letters have their own names, and each letter name represents both an uppercase letter symbol and a lowercase letter symbol.

Letter sounds knowledge

Letters represent sounds. This is true of both individual letters (e.g., 'S' represents /s/) and combinations of letters (e.g., 'Sh' represents /sh/). However, letter-sound relationships in English are not straightforward. Children must learn that one letter can represent multiple

sounds (e.g., 'G' makes the /g/ sound at the beginning of *get* and also the /j/ sound at the beginning of *gem*), and one sound can be represented by multiple letters (e.g., /s/ can be spelled with both 'S' and 'C').

Letter writing ability

Writing letters requires children to not only have knowledge of letter shapes, but also to have the visual memory and fine motor skills to reproduce letter shapes in written form.

Is alphabet knowledge sufficient for reading?

While knowing the alphabet is extremely important for supporting reading achievement, letter knowledge alone is not sufficient for children to become proficient readers. To develop strong reading skills, children need a great deal of additional knowledge, including:

- A large vocabulary
- Knowledge of grammatical rules
- Pragmatics (the social norms of language, e.g., how language use differs in spoken and written language)
- Listening comprehension (the ability to understand oral language)
- Phonological awareness (the ability to identify and manipulate units of oral language)
- Phonemic awareness (an awareness of the sounds of language)
- Verbal memory (memory for words and verbal items)
- Understanding of print concepts (e.g., knowing that text is read from left to right)

So while alphabet knowledge is the strongest predictor of reading achievement in the early school years, other skills should be nurtured along with alphabet knowledge in order to help children become strong readers.

An in-depth discussion of these skills is beyond the scope of this book. However, caring adults can do much to nurture the development of these skills simply by regularly sharing conversations, songs, rhymes, and books with children.

How do I teach the alphabet?

It is important to note that there are many letter learning opportunities in children's daily lives that do not require any special planning or set-up, and these opportunities provide powerful and effective ways of teaching the alphabet. For example:

Sing the alphabet song together. Initially the words won't have much meaning for your child, but over time your child will build connections between their emerging letter knowledge and the words of the song. Even older children may find the alphabet song useful, especially when they are working on alphabetic order tasks.

Point out letters and print in your child's environment. Read road signs and store banners to your child. Read menus at restaurants. If your child knows the first letter of their name, point it out when you see it in books, signs, and labels.

Label your child's possessions with their name. This helps your child learn letters that are particularly relevant and important to them. It also helps your child recognize that letters serve an important function in our lives.

These activities provide children with wonderful letter learning opportunities. However, many children benefit from more structured letter learning activities as well.

Below is a basic outline of children's developmental progression through learning the alphabet, along with suggested activities for children at each developmental stage.

Developing an initial understanding of print

At some point, children begin paying attention to specific features of print, such as the first letters of their names. They learn that we read print from left to right and from top to bottom. Children may also begin to produce letter-like forms and scribbles that are early attempts at writing. For many children, this happens between **ages 1 and 2**.

For children at this stage in their development, do activities that allow you to point out features of letters (e.g., "Look how this 'o' is shaped like a circle!") or name letters for your child (e.g., "You stacked the 'M' block on top of your tower!"). Provide opportunities for your child to develop their gross and fine motor skills. Sing songs and share rhymes that help your child develop their phonological awareness (the ability to identify and manipulate units of oral language) and phonemic awareness (the ability to focus on and manipulate the sounds of oral language).

Emerging letter knowledge

At the next developmental stage, children begin to identify some letters and make some letter-sound matches. Many children will begin to "write" using repeated wavy lines across a page with high and low points like letters. Children may also begin to write "words" with "squiggles" or with the letters they know.

For children at this stage, which often occurs between **ages 3 and 4**, focus on activities that promote letter recognition and letter sounds knowledge. Your child may also enjoy some multi-sensory letter writing activities (e.g., writing letters in shaving cream). If your child can form some letters, teach your child to write their name. Have your child dictate stories to you that you write down and they illustrate. Continue to sing songs and rhymes as well as provide opportunities for fine motor skills development.

Solidifying letter knowledge

Eventually, children begin to recognize all 26 letters and can identify most letter-sound matches. This typically occurs between **ages 5 and 6**. Children in this age range should also begin holding their pencil correctly with a three-finger (aka, "tripod") grip. Children who have developed these skills are ready for beginning reading instruction.

For children at this stage, engage them in activities to reinforce any letter sounds the child is struggling with, but most of the focus will be on letter formation and possibly letter case matching activities. Children at this stage are ready to begin early reading activities.

Guidelines for teaching the alphabet

Over the years, researchers and educators have identified teaching practices that lead to a more successful letter learning experience.

Do I teach letter names or letter sounds first?

Based on decades of research showing that letter naming knowledge is the single best predictor of children's reading growth,[1,2,3,7,14] you should either teach letter names *before* teaching letter sounds or *at the same time*.

Keep in mind that teaching letter names supports the learning of letter sounds, and many children do well learning letter names and letter sounds at the same time. You can do this very simply, such as by pointing to a letter and saying, "This letter is called 'J.' The 'J' says /j/. Can you say /j/? [Pause for response.] That's right, the 'J' says /j/."

Do I teach uppercase letters or lowercase letters first?

Educators do not all agree on whether to teach uppercase letters or lowercase letters first.

One reason to teach lowercase letters first is that more than 90% of the printed letters your child will encounter, particularly in books, will be lowercase letters. To facilitate reading, it may make sense to teach lowercase letters before uppercase letters.

On the other hand, uppercase letters have more straight lines, which makes them easier to write (e.g., 'E' vs. 'e'). Teaching uppercase letters first may help young children begin early writing activities sooner.

Ultimately, there is no right or wrong choice. Your child will eventually need to know both uppercase and lowercase letters. Start with what makes the most sense to you and what best aligns with the learning goals you have for your child.

In what order should I teach the letters?

The best order for teaching letters will depend on your teaching goals, and may vary depending on whether you are teaching letter names, letter sounds, or letter writing.

When teaching letter names and letter sounds, consider beginning with the first letter of the child's name. Then move on to teaching high-utility letters such as 'A,' 'C,' 'F,' 'G,' 'I,' 'M,' 'O,' 'R,' 'S,' and 'T.' (Low-utility letters like 'X' and 'Q' should be taught much later.) Knowing just six to eight high-utility letters allows a child to begin reading a number of simple two- and three-letter words.

When teaching letter sounds, it is easier to teach letters that make continuous sounds (sounds that can be prolonged or stretched out without distortion, such as /m/, /s/, and /a/) rather than letters that make stop sounds (sounds that cannot be prolonged or stretched out without distortion, such as /c/, /t/, and /b/).

Even though continuous sounds are easier, many high-utility letters have stop sounds. Therefore, you should feel free to introduce stop sounds early on. But if you find your child struggling with stop sounds, focus on continuous sounds for a few weeks and try introducing stop sounds again when your child may be more ready for them.

When teaching letters that make stop sounds, be sure to model using a quick /b/ or /d/ rather than saying /buh/ or /duh/. After all, when reading the words 'big' and 'dig' we do not say 'buh-ig' and 'duh-ig.'

When teaching children to write their letters, you may still wish to focus on high-utility letters or you may prefer to teach letters based on how easy they are to write. Letters with straight lines (e.g., 'E,' 'L') are easier to write than letters with curvy lines (e.g., 'S,' 'G').

See page 131 for sample letter sequences you can follow when teaching the alphabet.

To prevent confusion, avoid introducing letters that sound alike or look alike at the same time. For example, 'b' and 'd' look similar, and so should be introduced separately. See page 132 for a complete list of letter pairs that should be introduced separately.

How many letters should I introduce at a time?

Introduce new letters to your child at a reasonable pace, around two to four letters per week. Of course, this is just a guideline. The most important thing is that you follow your child's lead as they show you what they are ready for.

What letter style should I teach first: print, D'Nealian, or cursive?

The question of what letter style to teach first is a contentious one among educators, as print, D'Nealian, and cursive letters all have their ardent backers. In truth, each style has its advantages and disadvantages.

One significant advantage of teaching traditional print letters (also known as Zaner-Bloser letters) from the start is that the majority of the letters children encounter in books and other printed materials is written in this style. Among beginning writers, print letters also tend to be more legible.

In contrast to traditional print letters, D'Nealian letters are print letters written with a slant and a "tail" on the end. The D'Nealian style was designed with the goal of easing children's transition into cursive writing. However, research suggests that children transition equally well into cursive regardless of whether they first learn to write D'Nealian or print letters.[17] Children taught to write D'Nealian-style letters appear less likely to reverse their letters,[6] but they may commit more letter recognition errors.[11]

There are several reasons to consider teaching cursive first. With cursive, all of the lowercase letters are written beginning in the same place on the baseline. This is different than print and D'Nealian letters that start at various points depending on the letter. Further, spacing within and between words is more controlled. Because children are forced to lift their pencil at the end of every word, the beginning and ending of words may be more obvious. Children who write in cursive seem to have fewer problems with letter reversals as well.

All in all, there does not appear to be one "best" letter style to teach first. Interestingly, studies among older students have found that those who adopted a mixed letter style

incorporating both print and cursive elements wrote faster and more legibly than those who write in a strictly print style or a strictly cursive style.[9] Ultimately, you should select the style that best aligns with both your teaching goals and your child's learning needs.

How do I teach letters that make more than one sound?

There are many letters in the English alphabet that make more than one sound. All of the vowels, for example, make at least two sounds and several consonants do as well.

When teaching the vowels, begin by teaching the short vowel sounds. Your child will not need to learn the long vowel sounds until they have begun formal reading instruction and have mastered reading CVC (consonant-vowel-consonant) words, which use short vowel sounds. See page 133 for a description of short and long vowel sounds.

As for the consonants that make multiple sounds, start by teaching the most common sound, such as /g/ rather than /j/ for the letter 'G' and /c/ rather than /s/ for the letter 'C.' As with the vowels, your child will not need to learn the alternative sounds for these letters until they have mastered reading words using the most common sounds first.

Dealing with common challenges

Identifying letter shapes, learning letter names, learning letter sounds, and writing letters are all complex cognitive tasks requiring well-developed auditory, visual, and fine motor skills. These developmental processes take time to master, and there are common issues that arise as children work to master these skills.

Developing the proper pencil grip

The ability to correctly grasp a pencil with a three-finger grip (also known as the "tripod" grip) is something that develops over time. Many children do not acquire the necessary strength or fine motor control to use the three-finger grip until five or six years of age. This is because children need to develop the big muscles of their shoulders and arms before they are ready to develop the small muscles of their hands and fingers.

Children can develop the large muscles of the shoulders and arms by crawling, climbing, painting at an easel, throwing, and catching. Children can develop the small muscles of the hands and fingers by playing with blocks, picking up small objects, using play dough, cutting with scissors, threading beads, and coloring with crayons.

When children are forced to use the three-finger pencil grip before their large muscles are ready to support the grip, it can do them more harm than good. Therefore, it is best to allow your child to develop the correct pencil grip at their own pace. (See page 134 to learn more about the process of developing the pencil grip.) If your child is older than six and still having trouble, you may wish to seek advice from a teacher or occupational therapist who can suggest strategies to help your child.

Writing with the proper strokes

One obvious goal of writing instruction is to help children write legibly. But a second goal is to help children write quickly. Although writing speed may not be particularly important in the early grades, it matters as children get older. Research suggests students who use incorrect letter formation write more slowly, taking longer to complete written assignments and tests.[4]

Fortunately, teaching proper stroke order helps children write both legibly and quickly. In English, proper letter formation generally involves starting letter strokes at the top left and pulling the pencil down or to the right. Strokes that pull the pencil, as compared to strokes that push the pencil, minimize hand fatigue and reduce the chance that the paper will rip.

Another tip that supports quick and efficient writing is to teach children to write letters in one continuous stroke whenever possible. While some letters like 't' and 'j' require writers to lift the pencil from the paper to write a second stroke or dot, most letters can be written without lifting the pencil from the paper at all. Teaching the use of continuous strokes helps children become faster writers.

Children who are not yet ready to hold a pencil correctly can still practice proper letter formation through a variety of multi-sensory exercises, which can be found in Chapter 4.

Reversing letters

Most young children go through a period of reversing letters, writing 'b' instead of 'd' or mistaking 'u' for 'n.' The most common letter reversal children make is to confuse 'b' and 'd,' and it is not unusual for children to think that 'b,' 'd,' 'p,' and 'q' are all the same letter. After all, children know that a chair is still a chair even if you turn it upside down, so they must wonder why a 'd' becomes a 'p' just because it flips over!

These letter reversal errors do not usually indicate that the child has dyslexia or another reading disability. Instead, these errors seem to be a function of lack of experience with the letter, weak memory, and/or lack of left-right awareness. As such, most children outgrow these errors by the end of second or third grade.[5,8] Children who are still making reversal errors at the end of second or third grade should be assessed to determine if they could benefit from a targeted intervention.

If you observe your child reversing letters, gently correct your child. You may be able to decrease letter reversal errors by offering a variety of multi-sensory opportunities for practicing how to write them. For example, your child can practice writing letters in shaving cream (p. 103), tracing sandpaper letters (p. 82), poking holes in letters with a pin puncher (p. 90), or building letters with straws and play dough (p. 96).

Make letter learning a positive experience

You and your child will experience the most success with the activities in this book if you follow some basic guidelines:

Make learning relevant to your child

Making learning relevant to your child requires really knowing your child, understanding their interests, and being aware of what types of play they enjoy.

- Does your child have an interest in outer space? Create a space-themed sensory writing tray to practice letter formation (p. 105).

- Is your child always jumping around? Play a letter hop game to get them moving and learning letters at the same time (p. 58).
- Does your child love toy cars? Have your child practice letter formation by driving toy cars on roads shaped like letters (p. 81).
- Has your child recently learned to use scissors? Have them put those new skills to work by cutting up alphabet strips (p. 53).

Make learning fun and playful

The success of any activity depends in large part on the attitude you bring to it. Be sure your attitude conveys:

- Enthusiasm about the activity
- A readiness to have fun (acting serious or businesslike can stress your child out)
- Cheerful acceptance of mistakes (gently correct mistakes in a way that builds your child up rather than makes them feel ashamed or unintelligent)

Make learning a multi-sensory experience

Children (and grownups too!) learn best through multi-sensory experiences. Learning the alphabet should involve seeing letters, hearing letters, touching letters, building letters with various materials, and writing letters on different surfaces.

Children like to get their hands on things. They also need to move. In this book you will find activities that let children poke, pound, wrap, cut, swat, paint, and squirt letters.

It's time to get started!

With this book you now have 101 ideas at your fingertips to make letter learning fun, engaging, and successful. Enjoy your child's alphabet learning process, and take pride in knowing that you are setting your child up for a lifetime of reading success.

"Play is our brain's favorite way of learning." – Diane Ackerman

References

1.   Adams, M. J. (1990). *Beginning to read: Thinking and learning about print*. Cambridge, MA: The MIT Press.

2.   Bond, G. L., & Dykstra, R. (1967). The cooperative research program in first-grade reading instruction. *Reading Research Quarterly*, 2(4), 5–142.

3.   Chall, J. S. (1967). *Learning to read: The great debate*. New York: McGraw-Hill.

4.   Connelly, V., Dockrell, J., & Barnett, J. (2005). The slow handwriting of undergraduate students constrains overall performance in exam essays. *Educational Psychology*, 25, 99-107.

5.   Davidson, H. P. (1935). A study of the confusing letters B, D, P, and Q. *Journal of Genetic Psychology*, 47, 458-468.

6.   Farris, P. J. (1982). A comparison of handwriting strategies for primary grade students. Arlington, VA: *ERIC Document Reproduction Service* (CS 209 360).

7.   Foulin, J. N. (2005). Why is letter-name knowledge such a good predictor of learning to read? *Reading and Writing*, 18, 129-155.

8.   Gibson, E. J., Gibson, J. J., Pick, A. D., & Osser, H. A. (1962). A developmental study of the discrimination of letter-like forms. *Journal of Comparative and Physiological Psychology*, 55, 897-906.

9.   Graham, S., Weintraub N., & Berminger, V. W. (1998). The relationship between handwriting style and speed and legibility. *The Journal of Educational Research*, 91(5), 290-296.

10.   Hiebert, E. H., Pearson, P. D., Taylor, B. M., Richardson, V. & Paris, S. G. (1998). *Every Child a Reader: Applying Reading Research in the Classroom*. Ann Arbor, MI: CIERA.

11.   Kuhl, D. & Dewitz, P. (2001). The effect of handwriting style on alphabet recognition. In *Handwriting research: A guide to curriculum planning* (130-139). Columbus, OH: Zaner-Bloser.

12.   Mason, J. M. (1984). Early reading from a developmental perspective. In P. D. Pearson, R. Barr, M. L. Kamil, & P. Mosenthal (Eds.), *Handbook of Reading Research* (pp. 505-543). New York: Longman.

13.   Piasta, S., & Wagner, R. (2010). Learning letter names and sounds: Effects of instruction, letter type, and phonological processing skill. *Journal of Experimental Child Psychology*, 105, 324-344.

14.   Scanlon, D. M., & Vellutino, F. R. (1996). Prerequisite skills, early instruction, and success in first grade reading: Selected results from a longitudinal study. *Mental Retardation and Developmental Disabilities Research Review*, 2, 54-63.

15.   Snow, C. E., Burns, M. S., & Griffin, P. (Eds.). (1998). *Preventing reading difficulties in young children*. Washington, D.C.: National Academies Press.

16.   Strickland, D., & Schickedanz, J. A. (2004). *Learning about print in preschool: Working with letters, words, and beginning links with phonemic awareness*. Newark, DE: International Reading Association.

17.   Trap-Porter, J., Cooper, J. O., Hill, D. S., Swisher, K., & LaNunziata, L. J. (1984). D'Nealian and Zaner-Bloser manuscript alphabets and initial transition to cursive handwriting. *The Journal of Educational Research*, 77(6), 343-345.

101 Ways
to **Teach** the
Alphabet

CHAPTER TWO

. . . .

Activities That Teach
Letter Recognition

Play Dough Letter Stamping

Good activity for:

- Engaging children who love play dough
- Strengthening finger muscles

Materials needed:

- Play dough
- Letter stamps

Directions:

Provide your child with a ball of play dough and some letter stamps.

Have your child flatten the ball into a pancake and use the stamps to make letters in the dough.

Alphabet Parking Lot

Good activity for:

- Engaging children who love toy cars

Materials needed:

- 2 or more toy cars
- Painter's tape
- Dot stickers 1 inch (2.5 cm) in diameter
- Marker

Directions:

Use strips of painter's tape to create a "parking lot" on the floor. Write letters on the dot stickers, then stick one letter dot in each parking space. Make matching letter dot stickers and place them on top of the cars. Underline letters that can be easily confused (such as 'd' and 'p').

Show your child the parking lot and let them drive the cars around. Explain that each car has its own special parking spot marked with a letter.

Have your child park the cars by matching the letters on the cars with the letters in the parking spots.

Letter Creatures

Good activity for:

- Supporting children's creativity

Materials needed:

- *Letter Outlines* printable (p. 136)
- Art supplies (e.g., crayons, markers, googly eyes, glitter, yarn)
- Printer
- Printer paper
- Optional: Scissors

Directions:

Print the pages you need from the *Letter Outlines* printable.

Invite your child to get creative and turn the letter outlines into fun letter creatures using the available art supplies.

Letter Hunt Sensory Bin

Good activity for:

- Promoting sensory-rich play

Materials needed:

- Alphabet puzzle
- Small container
- Sensory filler (e.g., beans, rice, shredded paper, buttons)

Directions:

Fill a small container with your chosen sensory filler. Then remove the letters from the letter puzzle and bury them in the sensory bin.

Place the sensory bin next to the letter puzzle. Have your child find the letters in the bin and place them back into the letter puzzle.

Letter Bracelets

Good activity for:

- Engaging children who enjoy making wearable jewelry
- Developing fine motor skills

Materials needed:

- Letter beads
- Pipe cleaner
- Small tray

Directions:

Select a target letter. Place five to seven letter beads featuring the target letter on a tray along with several beads featuring other letters.

Provide your child with a pipe cleaner. Have them select only the letter beads with the target letter to put on the pipe cleaner, leaving the other beads on the tray.

When your child is done, help them twist the ends of the pipe cleaner together to make a bracelet for their wrist.

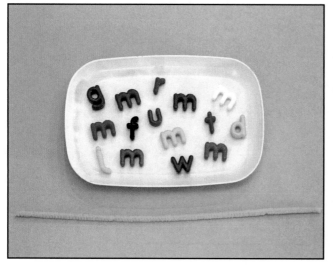

Sun Powered Letter Puzzle

Good activity for:

- Practicing letter matching skills
- Conducting a science demonstration showing the power of the sun

Materials needed:

- Construction paper (dark colors will provide the best results)
- Montessori movable alphabet letters
- Optional: Tray
- Sunshine

Directions:

Lay a sheet of construction paper in a sunny spot outdoors. Place the paper on a tray so you can move it easily if needed.

Have your child place several letters from the Montessori movable alphabet onto the sheet of paper. Leave the paper and letters in the sun for several hours until the exposed paper has sufficiently faded. Remove the letters from the paper to reveal the darker shapes left behind.

Have your child practice matching the Montessori movable alphabet letters to the letters on the paper.

Physical Attribute Letter Sort

Good activity for:

- Practicing sorting skills
- Drawing children's attention to the physical attributes of letters

Materials needed:

- Letter beads
- Container to hold unsorted letters
- Containers to hold sorted letters
- Labels describing how to sort letters

Directions:

Decide what attributes you want your child to sort the letters by, such as:

- letters with straight lines vs. curvy lines
- letters with holes vs. no holes
- letters with ascenders vs. descenders (must use lowercase letters for this sort)

Place the letters to be sorted in a container. Provide additional containers with labels where your child will put the sorted letters.

Show your child how to examine each letter and determine the appropriate container to put it in depending on its physical attributes.

Yarn Wrapped Letters

Good activity for:

- Developing fine motor skills
- Getting crafty

Materials needed:

- Thick cardstock
- Yarn
- Scissors
- Clear tape

Directions:

Cut letter shapes out of thick cardstock. Then cut pieces of yarn approximately 24-36 inches (60-90 cm) long. The shorter the yarn length, the less it will tangle, but the more pieces of yarn it will require to completely wrap a letter.

Tape one end of a piece of yarn to the letter you cut. Then hand the letter and yarn to your child.

Invite your child to wrap the yarn around the letter outline to create a beautiful yarn wrapped letter.

Blindfolded Letter Identification

Good activity for:

- Developing the stereognostic sense (ability to identify objects by touch)

Materials needed:

- Montessori movable alphabet letters
- Blindfold
- Bag to hold letters

Directions:

Introduce this activity only *after* your child has some familiarity with the alphabet, since this activity relies on your child identifying letter shapes using just their sense of touch.

Tie a blindfold around your child's eyes. Then place several letters from the Montessori movable alphabet into a bag.

Help your child reach into the bag and select one letter. Your child should use their fingers to feel the shape of the letter. Once they have guessed the letter, they should remove their blindfold to see if their guess was correct.

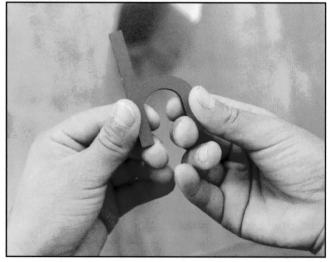

Letter Puzzles

Good activity for:

- Engaging children who like puzzles
- Exercising problem solving skills

Materials needed:

- *Letter Puzzles* printable (p. 231)
- Scissors
- Printer
- Printer paper or cardstock
- Optional: Laminator

Directions:

Print the *Letter Puzzles* printable. For greater durability, print on cardstock and/or laminate the pages. Cut the puzzles apart.

Provide the puzzle pieces for one letter and have your child assemble them.

If your child is ready for a bigger challenge, provide them with the puzzle pieces for two or three letters all mixed together. Have your child sort the pieces and assemble the letter puzzles.

Gross Motor Skills Letter Hunt

Good activity for:

- Taking learning outside
- Developing gross motor skills

Materials needed:

- Montessori movable alphabet letters
- Optional: Scooter board

Directions:

Lay the letters out in a wide open space, such as a driveway or blacktop.

Name a letter for your child to find. Then give your child a physical task to do as they search for the letter.

For example, your child may search for letters while sitting on a scooter board. Or your child could crab walk or do cartwheels to get to the letters. Pick a gross motor activity that your child will enjoy.

Once your child finds the letter, have them bring it back to you. Then name another letter for them to go find.

Funky Fonts Letter Sorting

Good activity for:

- Showing children that the same letter can be written in many different ways

Materials needed:

- *Funky Fonts Letter Sorting* printable (p. 258)
- Printer
- Printer paper or cardstock
- Optional: Laminator
- Optional: Small container
- Optional: Sensory filler (e.g., beans, sand, buttons)

Directions:

Print the letter cards you need from the *Funky Fonts Letter Sorting* printable. For greater durability, print on cardstock and/or laminate the pages.

Now it is time to get creative! Spread the letters out on a table, hide the letters around the room, or bury them in a sensory bin filled with rice, beans, or buttons.

Your child's job is to collect the cards and sort them into letter groups. Assist your child if they have difficulty recognizing the letters written in certain fonts.

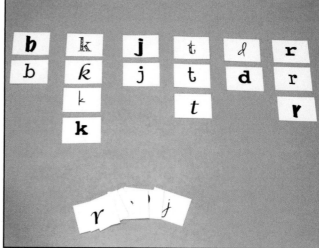

Miniature Letter Hunt

Good activity for:

- Engaging children who like using magnifying glasses

Materials needed:

- *Miniature Letter Hunt* printable (p. 287)
- Magnifying glass
- Printer
- Printer paper or cardstock
- Optional: Laminator
- Optional: Scissors

Directions:

Print the cards you need from the *Miniature Letter Hunt* printable. For greater durability, print on cardstock and/or laminate the pages. Cut the cards apart.

Each card has several teeny tiny letters on it that are difficult to read with the naked eye but can be easily read with the aid of a magnifying glass.

Encourage your child to search for miniature letters on the card using a magnifying glass.

Crayon Resist Letter Magic

Good activity for:

- Engaging children who enjoy painting
- Engaging children who love looking for hidden things

Materials needed:

- Watercolor paper
- Watercolor paint
- White crayon
- Optional: Paper
- Optional: Pencil

Directions:

Prepare the activity by writing several letters in white crayon on one or more pieces of white watercolor paper. The letters will not be easily visible.

Invite your child to add color to the paper using watercolor paints. The paper will absorb the paint, leaving the white letters visible as your child paints over them.

Let your child continue to paint until the entire paper is covered with color and they have found all the hidden letters.

Optionally, your child can record the letters they find on a separate piece of paper.

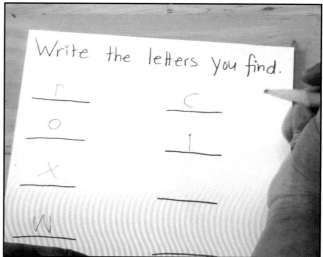

I Spy Letter Hunt

Good activity for:

- Supporting visual discrimination skills

Materials needed:

- Clear cylindrical container (e.g., empty water bottle)
- Letter beads
- Filler (e.g., rice, beans, shredded paper)
- Paper
- Crayon or pencil
- Optional: *I Spy. . . Letters* printable (p. 293)
- Optional: Printer

Directions:

Add alphabet beads to your clear container. As you add letters, write them on a sheet of paper (or use the *I Spy. . .Letters* printable).

Add filler material to your container until it is approximately 2/3 full. Do not overfill, as this will prevent the items from shifting as your child rotates the container.

Have your child search for letters in the I Spy container and cross them off the list as they find them.

Encourage your child to continue searching for letters until they have crossed off all of the letters on their list.

Spin and Touch the Letter

Good activity for:

- Playing with two or more children
- Getting children moving

Materials needed:

- Sturdy paper plate
- Marker
- Optional: Ruler (to draw straight lines)
- Paper fastener
- Paper clip
- 24 note cards
- Painter's tape

Directions:

Draw lines to divide a paper plate into four quarters. Label the quarters *left hand*, *right hand*, *left foot*, and *right foot*. Divide each quarter into four wedges. Label each wedge with a different letter, repeating the same four letters in each quarter. Press a paper fastener through the center of the plate, and slide a paper clip onto the fastener.

Make six note cards for each letter on the plate, writing one letter on each card. You will have a total of 24 note cards when finished. Tape them to the ground in straight lines. Spin the paper clip. Direct your child to touch the selected letter with the indicated hand or foot.

Animal Alphabet Do-a-Dot Trails

Good activity for:

- Supporting visual tracking skills

Materials needed:

- *Animal Alphabet Do-a-Dot Trails* printable (p. 296)
- Dot markers
- Printer
- Printer paper

Directions:

Print the worksheets you need from the *Animal Alphabet Do-a-Dot Trails* set. Pair a worksheet with a dot marker and present it to your child.

Show your child the target letter they need to follow along the do-a-dot trail. Have your child dot the starting circle with the dot marker. Then have your child find the adjacent circle with the target letter and dot it as well.

Your child should continue marking adjacent circles containing the target letter until they reach the end of the do-a-dot trail.

Mystery Letters

Good activity for:

- Developing the sense of touch
- Learning anytime and anywhere

Materials needed:

- Optional: Q-tip

Directions:

Have your child hold out their arm to you while closing their eyes. With your finger or a Q-tip, write a letter on your child's arm and have them guess which letter you wrote.

You might also give your child a chance to write letters on your arm for you to guess.

Continue playing for as long as your child is having fun.

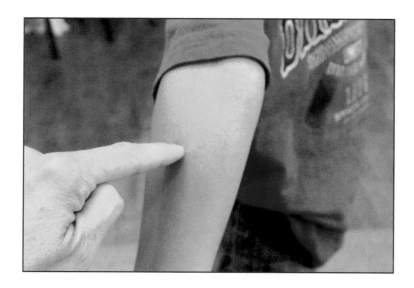

Letter Matching Memory Game

Good activity for:

- Developing visual memory

Materials needed:

- *Montessori Alphabet Tiles* printable (p. 375)
- Printer paper or cardstock
- Optional: Laminator
- Scissors

Directions:

Print and cut out two copies of the letter tiles you need from the *Montessori Alphabet Tiles* printable. For greater durability, print on cardstock and/or laminate the tiles.

Keep one set of letter tiles with you. Scatter another set on a table in a separate room.

Show your child a letter. Then hold on to the letter while your child goes to the other room and brings back the matching letter.

Your child should compare whether the letter they brought back matches the one you showed them. If they do not match, have your child try again.

Letter Graphing

Good activity for:

- Practicing graphing skills

Materials needed:

- *Letter Graphing* printable (p. 378)
- Optional: Pocket cube
- Optional: Dot marker
- Optional: Pencil
- Printer
- Printer paper
- Scissors

Directions:

Print the pages you need from the *Letter Graphing* printable, including one of the pages needed to make a letter die. Assemble the die.

Have your child roll the die.

Depending on which version of the *Letter Graphing* worksheet you printed, your child can use a dot marker to show how many times the letter has been rolled, or your child can write the letter in the box each time it is rolled.

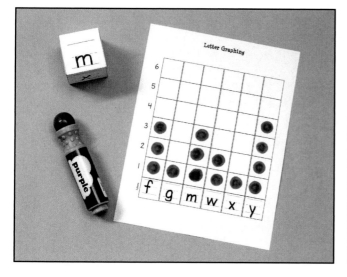

Letter Patterns

Good activity for:

- Practicing pattern recognition

Materials needed:

- *Letter Patterns* printable (p. 383)
- Optional: Pencil, crayon, or marker
- Optional: Letter tiles
- Optional: Letter stamps
- Printer
- Printer paper
- Optional: Scissors

Directions:

Print the worksheets you need from the *Letter Patterns* printable.

Have your child determine the pattern in each row and fill in the blank with the correct letter.

Your child can fill in the missing letter with a pencil, marker, letter tile, or letter stamp.

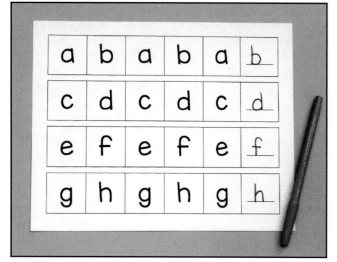

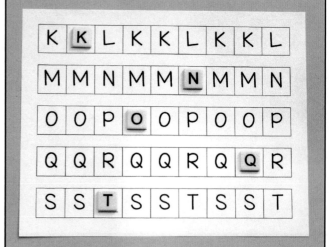

Color by Letter

Good activity for:

- Supporting visual discrimination skills
- Developing fine motor skills

Materials needed:

- *Color by Letter* printable (p. 433)
- Colored crayons, markers, or pencils
- Printer
- Printer paper

Directions:

Print the worksheets you need from the *Color by Letter* printable.

Have your child color in all the squares with the target letter.

When your child finishes coloring in the squares, they will notice that the colored squares form the uppercase letter corresponding to the lowercase letter they have been searching for.

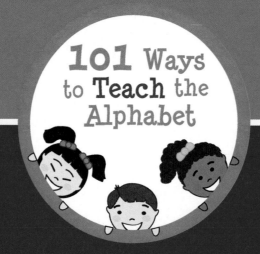

101 Ways to **Teach** the Alphabet

CHAPTER THREE

• •

Activities that Teach Letter Sounds

Alphabet Zip Line

Good activity for:

- Developing fine motor skills
- Learning in a fun and creative way

Materials needed:

- *Montessori Alphabet Tiles* printable (p. 375)
- String
- Paper clip
- Printer paper or cardstock
- Optional: Laminator
- Scissors

Directions:

Print and cut the letter tiles you need from the *Montessori Alphabet Tiles*. For greater durability, print on cardstock and/or laminate the tiles.

Set up your zip line by connecting a string from a high location your child can access (e.g., top of stairs) to a lower location.

Sit with your child at the top of the zip line with the letter tiles. Say a letter sound (e.g., /ĕ/). Your child should find the correct letter and hang it from the zip line with a paper clip. Once the letter is on the line, your child should release it and watch it slide down.

Pound the Sound

Good activity for:

- Developing fine motor skills
- Engaging children who love hammering

Materials needed:

- Cardboard box or large brick of polystyrene foam at least 5 inches (12 cm) thick
- Dot stickers 1 inch (2.5 cm) in diameter
- Marker
- Golf tees
- Child-friendly, lightweight hammer
- Protective eye gear

Directions:

Write letters on the dot stickers, underlining letters that can be easily confused (such as 'd' and 'p'). Stick the letters on top of the box, spread out in a random pattern. Make sure the box is taller than the golf tees to avoid damage to the surface underneath.

Have your child put on protective eye gear.

Say a letter sound (e.g., /p/). Have your child find the correct letter and hammer a golf tee into it.

Alphabet Soup

Good activity for:

- Promoting sensory-rich play
- Engaging budding chefs who enjoy kitchen-related pretend play

Materials needed:

- Letter tiles
- Large pot
- Stirring spoon
- "Ingredients" to make the "soup," such as shaving cream, food coloring, water, leaves, or grass
- Optional: Apron or smock to protect children's clothing

Directions:

Set out a large pot along with a stirring spoon, some letter tiles, and any "ingredients" you have selected. Explain to your child that they will be making alphabet soup.

Invite your child to add ingredients to the pot. Let them stir the ingredients with the spoon as if they were making soup.

Then invite your child to add letters to make alphabet soup. Have your child identify the sound each letter makes before adding it to the soup.

Letter Squish

Good activity for:

- Promoting tactile sensory play

Materials needed:

- White glue
- Shaving cream
- Mixing bowl
- Mixing spoon
- Tray
- Marker

Directions:

In a large bowl, mix together approximately equal parts white glue and shaving cream. Drop 26 large dollops of the mixture onto a tray. Allow the puffs to dry overnight, then use a marker to write a letter on each one. When properly prepared, the puffy letters will quickly bounce back to their original shape when squished.

Say a letter sound (e.g., /s/). Your child should find the correct letter and squish it with their fingers or smash it with their fist. You can also remove the letter puffs from the tray and put them on the floor for your child to stomp with their feet.

Alphabet Cutting Strips

Good activity for:

- Developing scissor skills

Materials needed:

- *Alphabet Cutting Strips* printable (p. 460)
- Child-friendly scissors
- Adult scissors
- Printer
- Printer paper

Directions:

Print and prepare the cutting strips you need from the *Alphabet Cutting Strips* printable according to the directions.

Provide the strips to your child along with a pair of child-friendly scissors. Have your child cut the letters and images apart along the dotted lines.

Encourage your child to say the sound each letter makes and to name each object as they cut apart the strips.

Fold the Flaps

Good activity for:

- Developing fine motor skills

Materials needed:

- Paper plate
- Marker
- Scissors

Directions:

Write letters around the outside edge of a paper plate. Underline letters that can be easily confused (such as 'd' and 'p'). Then use scissors to make small cuts between the letters so that each letter is written on its own flap.

Hand the plate to your child. Say a letter sound (e.g., /f/). Your child should find the correct letter and fold that flap down.

Continue playing until your child has folded down all of the letter flaps.

Starry Night Letters

Good activity for:

- Engaging children who love stickers
- Teaching children about the night sky

Materials needed:

- Black construction paper
- Foam star stickers
- Permanent marker
- Optional: White chalk

Directions:

Use a permanent marker to write letters on several star stickers. Underline letters that can be easily confused (such as 'd' and 'p').

Explain to your child that the black paper is the night sky, but the stars are missing.

Say a letter sound (e.g., /s/). Your child should find the star with the correct letter and add it to the night sky.

Continue until the sky is filled with beautiful letter stars. Once your child has placed the stars in the "sky," your child may wish to form constellations by drawing lines between the stars using white chalk.

Swat the Fly

Good activity for:

- Getting children up and moving

Materials needed:

- *Swat the Fly* printable (p. 487)
- Fly swatter
- Painter's tape
- Printer
- Printer paper or cardstock
- Optional: Laminator
- Scissors

Directions:

Print and prepare the letter cards you need from the *Swat the Fly* printable according to the printable directions. For greater durability, print on cardstock and/or laminate the pages.

Stick several fly letter cards to the wall using painter's tape.

Hand your child a fly swatter. Then say a letter sound (e.g., /f/). Your child should find the fly with the correct letter and use the fly swatter to "swat" the fly.

Magic Disappearing Letters

Good activity for:

- Strengthening the pincer grasp
- Connecting letter learning to the science of chromatography

Materials needed:

- Coffee filter
- Marker
- Pipette
- Small container of water
- Tray to contain mess

Directions:

Use a marker to write several letters on the coffee filter, leaving plenty of blank space between them. Place the filter on a tray along with the water and pipette.

Show your child how to fill the pipette with water by squeezing the bulb, dipping the tip into the water, and then gently releasing the bulb to draw the water into the pipette before removing it from the water.

Say a letter sound (e.g., /p/). Your child should find the correct letter and drip a few drops of water on it. Watch as the letter magically disappears due to the process of chromatography.

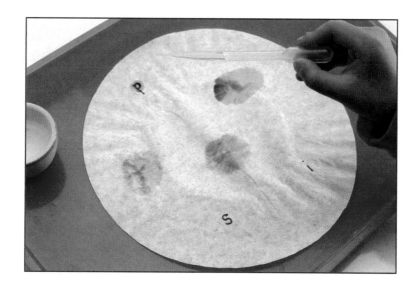

Letter Hop

Good activity for:

- Developing gross motor skills
- Getting children up and moving

Materials needed:

- Sticky notes
- Marker

Directions:

Write several letters on sticky notes and scatter them on the floor in an open area.

Say a letter sound (e.g., /h/). Your child should find the correct letter and hop over to it.

Continue saying letter sounds and having your child hop from one letter to the next for as long as your child is having fun.

Squirt the Letter

Good activity for:

- Taking learning outside
- Developing hand-eye coordination

Materials needed:

- Water gun
- Chalk
- Wall, fence, or other surface to write letters on

Directions:

Use chalk to write several letters on a wall or fence.

Hand your child a water gun filled with water. Say a letter sound (e.g., /y/). Your child should find the correct letter and shoot it with water.

Continue until your child has had a chance to shoot water at all the letters.

Cotton in the Cups

Good activity for:

- Engaging children who love a physical challenge

Materials needed:

- 2 or more disposable cups
- Permanent marker
- Cotton balls

Directions:

Use a permanent marker to write letters on the disposable cups. Place the cups in a line with the letters facing your child. Have your child stand or sit a short distance from the cups. Give your child some cotton balls.

Say a letter sound (e.g., /c/). Your child should try to throw a ball of cotton in the cup marked with the correct letter.

Alternatively, turn the cups so that your child cannot see the letters. Have your child throw a cotton ball into a cup, then look at the letter on the cup the ball landed in and say the sound it makes.

Letter Pop

Good activity for:

- Engaging children who love popping balloons

Materials needed:

- Balloons
- Painter's tape
- Permanent marker
- Optional: Wood handled pin puncher

Directions:

Blow up several balloons, then use a permanent marker to write one letter on each balloon. Use painter's tape to attach the balloons to the wall.

Invite your child over. Say a letter sound (e.g., /p/). Your child should find the balloon with the correct letter and pop it.

Your child can pop the balloon by poking it with a wood handled pin puncher or by removing it from the wall and sitting on it.

Continue until all the balloons have been popped.

Spot It and Dot It

Good activity for:

- Engaging children who love dot markers

Materials needed:

- *Spot It and Dot It* printable (p. 494)
- Dot markers
- Printer
- Printer paper

Directions:

Print the worksheets you need from the *Spot It and Dot It* printable.

Have your child identify the initial sound of the object in the upper right corner of the page. Then have your child determine which letter makes that sound.

For example, rainbow starts with /r/ which is made by the letter 'r.'

Your child should then "spot and dot" all instances of that letter on the page, marking the circles with a dot marker.

Life-Size Alphabet Board Game

Good activity for:

- Encouraging children to be physically active
- Playing with two or more children

Materials needed:

- Sticky notes
- Marker
- Large die made from a pocket cube with numbers inserted into the pockets (or simply use a regular die)

Directions:

Create a life-size alphabet board game by writing letters on 10 to 20 sticky notes and placing them in a large circle on the floor. You can have repeat letters if needed. Underline letters that can be easily confused (such as 'd' and 'p').

Prepare your die, either using numbers inserted into a pocket cube or a regular die.

Have your child pick a letter to start on and roll the die. Your child should move forward the indicated number of spaces, saying the sound of each letter as they step on it.

Play for as long as everyone is having fun.

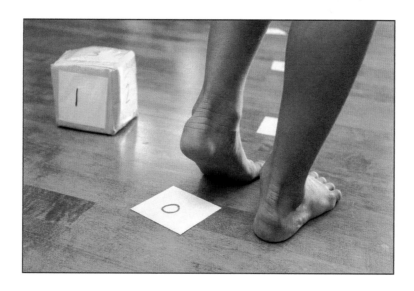

Beginning Sounds Clip Cards

Good activity for:

- Developing fine motor skills
- Providing children with self-correcting learning tasks (control of error)

Materials needed:

- *Beginning Sounds Clip Cards* printable (p. 547)
- Clothespins
- Scissors
- Printer
- Printer paper or cardstock
- Optional: Laminator

Directions:

Print the clip cards you need from the *Beginning Sounds Clip Cards* printable. For greater durability, print on cardstock and/or laminate the pages.

Have your child use a clothespin to clip the letter that makes the beginning sound of the object pictured.

To make this activity self-correcting, put a dot on the back of each clip card to indicate which letter is the correct answer. This will allow your child to check their answer by flipping the card over after clipping it with the clothespin.

Letter Kaboom

Good activity for:

- Playing with two or more children
- Engaging children who love games

Materials needed:

- Jumbo craft sticks
- Permanent marker
- Container to hold craft sticks

Directions:

Write letters on one end of the craft sticks with a permanent marker. Underline letters that can be easily confused (such as 'd' and 'p'). For every four or five sticks with a letter, make one stick that says "Kaboom!" Put the sticks into a container with the blank ends facing up.

Players take turns selecting a stick. Players must say the letter sound to keep the stick. Otherwise, the stick gets returned to the container. When a player draws a "Kaboom!" stick, that player must return all of their sticks. End the game after a set amount of time. The player with the most sticks wins.

Beginning Sounds Bingo

Good activity for:

- Playing with two or more children
- Engaging children who love Bingo games

Materials needed:

- *Beginning Sounds Bingo* printable (p. 566)
- Small objects to mark spaces on the Bingo card (e.g., coins, pebbles)
- Printer
- Printer paper or cardstock
- Optional: Laminator
- Scissors

Directions:

Print the pages you need from the *Beginning Sounds Bingo* printable. For greater durability, print on cardstock and/or laminate the pages.

Decide ahead of time how the game will be won, either by completing an entire row, completing an entire column, or completing the entire card (blackout).

Turn over a letter card and say the sound it makes. Have your child place a small object on the picture beginning with that letter sound. Continue playing until someone gets a Bingo.

Letter Hockey

Good activity for:

- Engaging children who love a physical challenge

Materials needed:

- A small goal (made from blocks, cardboard, etc.)
- Several milk caps, cleaned and dried
- Permanent marker

Directions:

Use a marker to write letters on the milk caps. Underline letters that can be easily confused (such as 'd' and 'p'). Then help your child build a small goal for the activity using any materials you have on hand. Place the goal on smooth surface like a table top or hard floor.

Give your child the milk caps. Say a letter sound (e.g., /m/). Your child should find the milk cap with the correct letter and use their fingers to flick it across the floor or table into the goal.

Roll the Tube

Good activity for:

- Fidgety kids who like to hold objects in their hands

Materials needed:

- Cardboard tube (e.g., paper towel roll)
- Marker

Directions:

Draw a spiral line around a cardboard tube. Write letters along the spiral line, leaving approximately 2 inches (5 cm) of space between each letter.

Have your child hold the tube. Starting with the letter on the far left side, your child should spin the tube and say the sound made by each letter along the spiral. Have your child trace the spiral with their finger if needed.

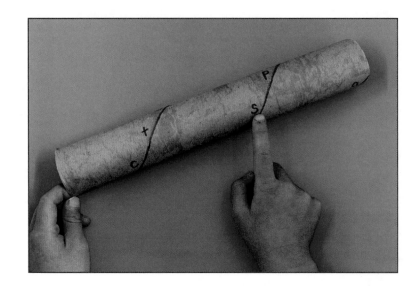

Put a Sticker on the Sound

Good activity for:

- Developing fine motor skills
- Engaging children who love stickers

Materials needed:

- *Put a Sticker on the Sound* printable (p. 581)
- Dot stickers 1 inch (2.5 cm) in diameter
- Marker
- Printer
- Printer paper

Directions:

Print the worksheets you need from the *Put a Sticker on the Sound* printable.

Use a marker to write letters on dot stickers that correspond with the images on the pages you have printed.

Invite your child to name each picture on the page and identify the initial sound of the word. For example, 'cow' starts with the /c/ sound.

Then have your child find the dot sticker beginning with that letter sound and place it on the worksheet, either on top of or right next to the picture.

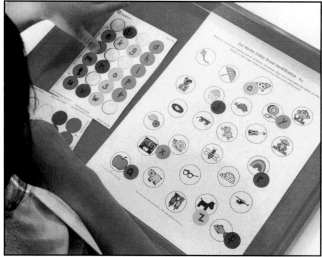

Alphabet Dominoes

Good activity for:

- Providing children with self-correcting learning tasks (control of error)

Materials needed:

- *Alphabet Dominoes* printable (p. 586)
- Scissors
- Printer
- Printer paper or cardstock
- Optional: Laminator

Directions:

Print and prepare the domino sets you need from the *Alphabet Dominoes* printable according to the printable directions. For greater durability, print on cardstock and/or laminate the dominoes.

Have your child find the starting domino marked by a green dot. Your child should lay the domino on a work surface and identify the initial sound of the object pictured. Then your child should find a domino with a letter that matches the sound from the first domino and lay it just to the right. Your child should continue placing dominoes until they reach the last domino, marked with a red dot.

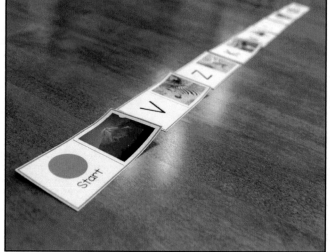

Letter Hopscotch

Good activity for:

- Taking learning outside
- Promoting physical activity

Materials needed:

- Sidewalk chalk
- Open area of concrete or asphalt

Directions:

Use sidewalk chalk to draw large boxes on an open area of concrete or asphalt. A typical hopscotch course alternates between one or two single boxes followed by a double box. Make a total of eight to ten boxes. Write a letter in each box.

Have your child start at the beginning. They should hop from one box to the next, saying the sound each letter makes as they land on it.

Keep the activity fresh and fun by having your child jump forwards, then backwards, and then sideways. You can also challenge your child to jump with one or two feet.

Snowman Letter Sounds Matching

Good activity for:

- Learning letter sounds in wintertime

Materials needed:

- *Snowman Letter Sounds Matching* printable (p. 606)
- Scissors
- Printer
- Printer paper or cardstock
- Optional: Laminator

Directions:

Print the pages you need from the *Snowman Letter Sounds* printable. For greater durability, print on cardstock and/or laminate the pages.

Have your child select a snowman head and identify the sound made by the letter. Then have your child find the two images beginning with that letter sound to make the rest of the snowman's body.

Your child should put all three pieces together to create a snowman.

Letter Sounds All Around

Good activity for:

- Getting children up and moving

Materials needed:

- Sticky notes
- Marker

Directions:

Prepare the activity by writing letters on sticky notes.

Invite your child to select one sticky note and find an object in the environment (e.g., home, classroom, yard) starting with the sound made by that letter. Your child should attach the sticky note to the object, then return to you for another letter.

Be supportive of creative letter-sound pairings, such as 'y' for a 'yellow' ball or 'f' for a 'fuzzy' blanket.

Miniature Objects Sound Sorting

Good activity for:

- Engaging children who enjoy playing with miniature objects

Materials needed:

- Montessori movable alphabet letters
- Miniature objects

Directions:

Set several letters out on a work surface. Give your child a container of miniature objects starting with sounds matching those of the letters you have laid out.

Have your child pick up one object, identify its initial sound, and place it in a line under the correct letter.

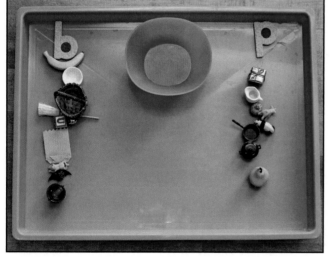
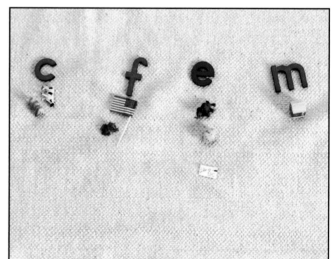

Letters in the Mail

Good activity for:

- Engaging children who love to send and receive mail

Materials needed:

- Mailbox (any box can be used)
- Note cards
- Envelopes
- Markers

Directions:

Turn any box into a mailbox for sending and receiving letters.

On a note card, write one letter. Underline letters that can be easily confused (such as 'd' and 'p'). Place the letter into an envelope and stick it in the mailbox for your child.

Allow your child to retrieve the mail. They should open the envelope and "read" the card by saying the sound the letter makes.

Encourage your child to write their own letter on a card and mail it back to you.

DIY Alphabet Photo Book

Good activity for:

- Engaging children who love taking pictures

Materials needed:

- Camera
- Environment with a variety of objects
- Printer
- Printer paper or cardstock
- Stapler or other book binding tool

Directions:

Hand your child a camera and invite them to photograph objects that represent each letter of the alphabet.

For example, your child might photograph an apple for 'A,' a cat for 'C,' a mop for 'M,' or a pillow for 'P.'

When your child is done taking photos, print the pictures and assemble them into an alphabet photo book for your child to continue enjoying.

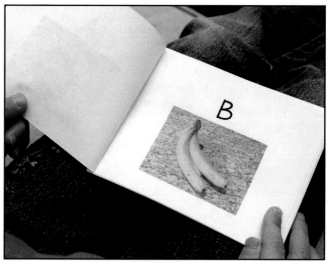

Guess the Hidden Letter

Good activity for:

- Engaging children who love guessing games

Materials needed:

- 2 or more cups
- Montessori movable alphabet letters
- Miniature objects

Directions:

Turn the cups upside down, and hide one letter under each of them. On top of each cup, place a miniature object whose initial sound matches the hidden letter. Then invite your child over.

Have your child identify the initial sound of the object on the cup. Then have your child determine which letter makes that sound.

Your child should then lift the cup to reveal the letter and see if their guess was correct.

Continue until your child has looked under every cup.

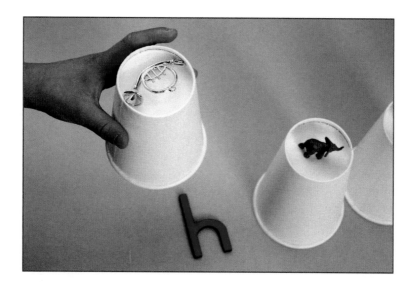

Muffin Tin Letter-Sound Matching

Good activity for:

- Engaging children who enjoy playing with miniature objects

Materials needed:

- Montessori movable alphabet letters
- Miniature objects starting with different letter sounds
- Muffin tin

Directions:

Gather a variety of miniature objects, and place one into each cup of a muffin tin.

Have your child identify the initial sound of each object. Then, your child should pick the letter that makes that sound and add it to the muffin cup.

Continue until your child has placed one letter in each cup of the muffin tin next to each miniature object.

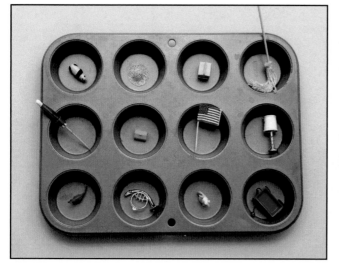
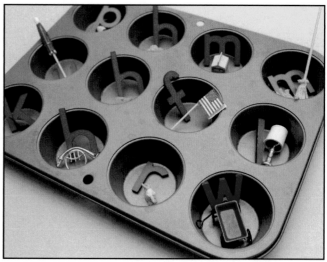

Spin a Letter, Say a Word

Good activity for:

- Playing with two or more children
- Stimulating children's creative thinking skills

Materials needed:

- Sturdy paper plate
- Marker
- Optional: Ruler (to draw straight lines)
- Paper fastener
- Paper clip

Directions:

Draw lines to divide a paper plate into four or more wedge-shaped sections. Label each section with a different letter. Underline letters that can be easily confused (such as 'd' and 'p').

Press a paper fastener through the center of the plate, and slide a paper clip onto the fastener. Your spinner is now ready.

To play, each player takes a turn spinning the paper clip. When the spinner lands on a letter, the player should name a word beginning with that letter sound.

101 Ways to Teach the Alphabet

CHAPTER FOUR

· ·

Activities That Teach Letter Formation

Road Letters

Good activity for:

- Engaging children who love toy cars

Materials needed:

- *Road Letters* printable (p. 625)
- Toy car
- Printer
- Printer paper or cardstock
- Optional: Laminator

Directions:

Print the pages you need from the *Road Letters* printable. For greater durability, print on cardstock and/or laminate the pages.

Invite your child to race a toy car along the letter-shaped road.

Montessori Sandpaper Letters

Good activity for:

- Supporting tactile learning

Materials needed:

- Montessori sandpaper letters

Directions:

Sandpaper letters (cards with an embossed sandpaper letter on them) are an important learning tool in Montessori classrooms. Sandpaper letters allow children to literally feel the shape of a letter as they run their finger over the card.

Hand your child a sandpaper letter. Say the letter's name and the sound it makes (e.g., /n/). Have your child repeat after you.

Then have your child trace the letter using their pointer finger, drawing the strokes in the same order they would use to write the letter on paper.

Alphabet Play Dough Mats

Good activity for:

- Promoting sensory-rich play
- Promoting creativity
- Developing fine motor skills

Materials needed:

- *Alphabet Play Dough Mats* printable (p. 730)
- Play dough
- Printer
- Printer paper or cardstock
- Laminator or plastic cover

Directions:

Print the mats you need from the *Alphabet Play Dough Mats* printable.

Laminate the play dough mats (or insert them into a plastic cover) so the play dough will not stick to the pages.

Have your child use play dough to form the letters on each mat. Then have them use play dough to perform the suggested action on each page.

Show the fish blowing bubbles.

Add some eggs to the nest.

Letter Rubbings

Good activity for:

- Developing fine motor skills

Materials needed:

- Montessori movable alphabet letters
- Crayons with the paper removed
- Tracing paper or printer paper

Directions:

Provide your child with crayons, paper, and several letters from the Montessori movable alphabet.

Show your child how to place a letter under the paper and rub the side of the crayon gently over the paper to make a letter rubbing.

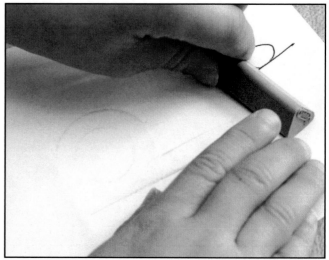

Sensory Nature Letters

Good activity for:

- Using natural materials for learning
- Getting crafty

Materials needed:

- *Letter Outlines* printable (p. 136)
- Natural materials such as rocks, leaves, acorns, flower petals, twigs, etc.
- Glue
- Printer
- Printer paper or cardstock
- Optional: Scissors

Directions:

Print the pages you need from the *Letter Outlines* printable.

Invite your child to glue on natural materials in order to decorate each letter outline.

Once the glue dries, your child may enjoy tracing the materials with their finger or hanging their artwork on the wall.

Dot Letters

Good activity for:

- Developing fine motor skills

Materials needed:

- *Dot Letter Activity Pages* printable (p. 757)
- Optional: Dot markers
- Optional: Dot stickers 1 inch (2.5 cm) in diameter
- Optional: Pom poms
- Optional: Glass gems
- Optional: Googly eyes
- Printer
- Printer paper or cardstock
- Optional: Laminator

Directions:

Print the letter pages you need from the *Dot Letter Activity Pages* printable. If you plan to reuse the pages, print on cardstock and/or laminate them for greater durability.

Invite your child to fill in all of the dots on the letter using dot markers, dot stickers, pom poms, glass gems, googly eyes, or any other craft supplies you have on hand.

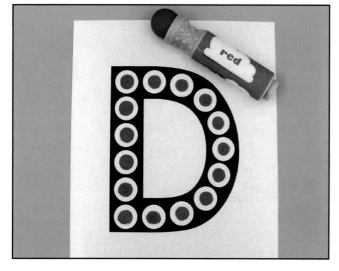

Yarn and Glue Letters

Good activity for:

- Getting crafty
- Making your own letter manipulatives

Materials needed:

- *Letter Outlines* printable (p. 136)
- Yarn pieces 5-10 inches long (12-24 cm)
- Glue
- Water
- Container (for mixing glue and water)
- Wax paper
- Painter's tape
- Tray
- Printer
- Printer paper

Directions:

Print the pages you need from the *Letter Outlines* printable. Use painter's tape to secure each page to a tray. Place wax paper over each page and secure it to the tray with painter's tape as well.

In a small container, mix glue with a small amount of water until it is runny. Show your child how to dip the yarn into the glue mixture until it is completely soaked. Then have your child lay the gluey string on the wax paper, filling in each letter outline with the soaked yarn. Let the letters dry completely. This may take several days. Once dry, peel the letters from the wax paper and enjoy.

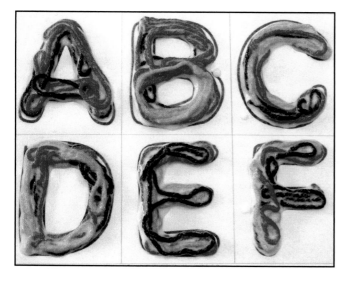

Aluminum Foil Letters

Good activity for:

- Developing fine motor skills

Materials needed:

- Montessori movable alphabet letters
- Aluminum foil

Directions:

Cut the aluminum foil into large squares that completely cover the letters in your Montessori movable alphabet set.

Have your child select a letter and cover it with a square of aluminum foil. Show your child how to use their fingers to press down on the foil so it wraps around the letter, creating an impression of it.

After your child picks up the foil, it should retain the shape of the letter.

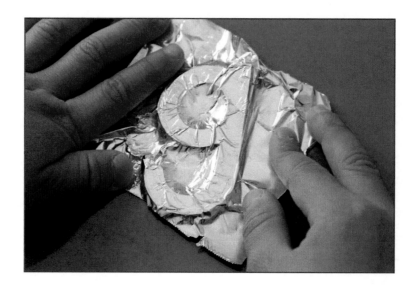

Button Letters

· ·

Good activity for:

- Developing fine motor skills
- Engaging children who love using glue

Materials needed:

- *Letter Outlines* printable (p. 136)
- Buttons
- Glue
- Printer
- Printer paper

Directions:

Print the pages you need from the *Letter Outlines* printable. Provide the letter outlines to your child along with buttons and glue.

Invite your child to fill in the letter outlines by gluing on buttons.

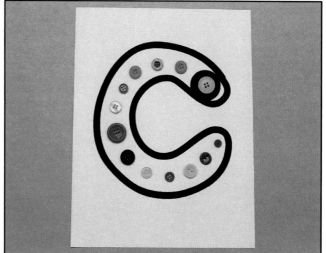

Letter Pin Punching

Good activity for:

- Practicing correct pencil grip

Materials needed:

- *Letter Pin Punching Pages* printable (p. 784)
- Wood handled pin puncher
- Thick felt mat
- Printer
- Printer paper or cardstock

Directions:

Print and cut the *Letter Pin Punching Pages* you need. Set one page on top of a thick felt mat.

Give your child the wood handled pin puncher. Invite your child to punch a hole in each circle that forms the letter.

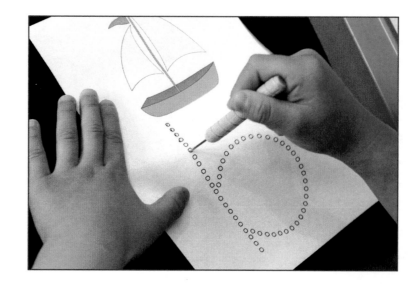

Letter Lacing

Good activity for:

- Developing fine motor skills
- Engaging children who love lacing activities

Materials needed:

- *Alphabet Lacing Cards* printable (p. 811)
- Yarn
- Scissors
- Tape
- Printer
- Printer paper or cardstock
- Optional: Laminator

Directions:

Print, cut, and punch holes in the *Alphabet Lacing Cards* you need. For greater durability, print the letters on cardstock and/or laminate the pages.

Cut a length of yarn approximately 10-12 inches (25-30 cm) longer than what your child should need. Wrap tape tightly around one end of the yarn to prevent it from fraying (as any fraying will make the lacing task more difficult).

Show your child how to lace the yarn in and out of the holes on the letter.

Q-tip Letter Erasing

Good activity for:

- Developing fine motor skills
- Practicing correct pencil grip

Materials needed:

- White board
- Dry erase marker
- Q-tip

Directions:

Write several letters on the white board with a dry erase marker. Invite your child over and hand them a Q-tip.

Name a letter and have your child find it on the white board. Invite your child to erase the letter by tracing it with the Q-tip.

Color the Letters

Good activity for:

- Learning colors
- Developing fine motor skills

Materials needed:

- *Color the Letters* printable (p. 840)
- Crayons or markers
- Printer
- Printer paper or cardstock
- Optional: Laminator
- Optional: Small container
- Optional: Sensory filler (e.g., beans, sand, buttons)

Directions:

Print and prepare the letter tracing worksheet and one set of letter tiles from the *Color the Letters* printable according to the directions. Gather crayons or markers in colors matching those on the letter tiles.

Place the letter tiles where your child can reach them, either in a pile on the table or hidden inside a sensory bin filled with beans, sand, or buttons.

Have your child select one letter tile at a time, identify the letter on the tile, and find the matching letter on the tracing worksheet. Your child should trace the letter in the same color shown on the letter tile.

Letter Poking and Sewing

Good activity for:

- Developing fine motor skills
- Engaging children who enjoy sewing

Materials needed:

- Cardstock
- Wood handled pin puncher
- Thick felt mat
- Large plastic needle
- Yarn
- Marker

Directions:

Use a marker to write a large letter on the cardstock. Place the letter on a felt mat and have your child poke holes in it with a wood handled pin puncher. Ideally, the holes should be spaced 1/2 inch (1.5 cm) apart.

Once your child has poked holes in the letter, show them how to thread the yarn through the eye of the needle. Then have your child "sew" the letter by inserting the needle in and out of the holes they poked.

 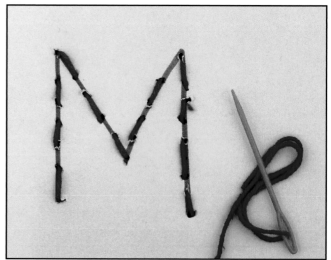

Q-tip Painted Letters

Good activity for:

- Developing fine motor skills
- Engaging children who love to paint

Materials needed:

- *Q-tip Painted Letter Pages* printable (p. 850)
- Q-tip
- Tempera paint
- Small container to hold the paint
- Printer
- Printer paper or cardstock
- Scissors

Directions:

Print and prepare the pages you need from the *Q-tip Painted Letter Pages* printable according to the printable directions. Squirt a small amount of paint into a container.

Invite your child to dip one end of the Q-tip into the paint and use it to fill in all the dots that form the letter.

Straw and Play Dough Letters

Good activity for:

- Developing fine motor skills
- Engaging children who love play dough

Materials needed:

- Play dough
- Plastic straws cut to 1 inch (2.5 cm) tall
- Optional: Montessori sandpaper letters

Directions:

Show your child how to roll a ball of play dough and flatten it into a pancake.

Once your child has made a play dough pancake, have them poke straws into the play dough to form a letter.

If your child needs help remembering the letter shapes, offer a set of Montessori sandpaper letters for reference.

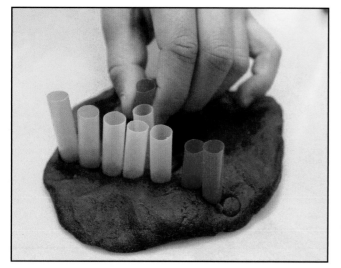

Cornstarch Block Letters

Good activity for:

- Getting crafty

Materials needed:

- Cornstarch blocks (e.g., biodegradable packing peanuts or Magic Nuudles)
- Sponge
- Container with small amount of water
- Optional: Cardboard to use as base for building

Directions:

Cornstarch blocks are non-toxic cylinders made from cornstarch. When slightly damp, they stick together and can be used to build all manner of structures.

Place a sponge into your water container. The top of the sponge should sit well above the top of the water.

Show your child how to build letters by wetting one end of the cornstarch block on the sponge and pressing it against another block until it sticks.

Encourage your child to build letters using this technique.

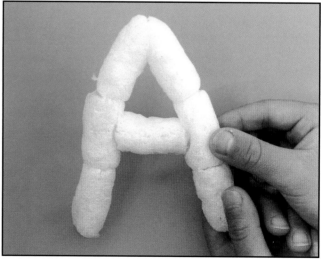

Kinetic Sand Letters

Good activity for:

- Promoting sensory-rich play

Materials needed:

- Kinetic sand
- Tray
- Optional: Montessori sandpaper letters

Directions:

Place a pile of kinetic sand on a tray.

Name a letter for your child to make. Have your child use kinetic sand to form the letter.

If your child needs help remembering the letter shapes, offer a set of Montessori sandpaper letters for reference.

Spaghetti Letters

Good activity for:

- Promoting sensory-rich play

Materials needed:

- Spaghetti that has been cooked and then cooled
- Bowl
- Water
- Optional: Tray to use as work surface
- Optional: Montessori sandpaper letters

Directions:

Note: This activity may not be safe for children with food allergies.

Cook the spaghetti, then rinse in cold water. Place the cooked spaghetti into a bowl. You may need to add water to the bowl so the spaghetti doesn't become too sticky.

Invite your child to select strands of spaghetti and use them to form letters. Your child can use their fingers to cut the strands into smaller pieces as needed.

If your child needs help remembering the letter shapes, offer a set of Montessori sandpaper letters for reference.

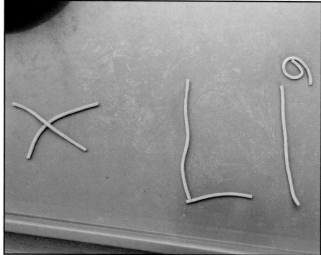

Tape Resist Letter Art

Good activity for:

- Combining letter learning and art

Materials needed:

- Painter's tape
- Paint brush
- Watercolor paints
- Watercolor paper

Directions:

Set out the materials and then invite your child over. Have your child use the painter's tape to make a letter on the paper.

Then have your child cover the entire sheet of paper with watercolor paints, painting right over the tape.

Let the paint dry. Then remove the painter's tape to reveal the letter underneath.

Consider displaying your child's beautiful artwork on a wall or bulletin board.

Crystallized Letters

Good activity for:

- Combining letter learning and the science of crystal formation

Materials needed:

- Pipe cleaners
- Salt
- Pot
- Stove
- Glass jar
- Craft stick (or pencil)
- String

Directions:

Have your child form a letter using pipe cleaners. Meanwhile, fill the pot with water and heat until it nears boiling. Stir salt into the water until no more salt will dissolve (~3 tablespoons of salt for every 1 cup of water). Pour the solution into a jar.

Tie one end of a string to your letter and the other end to a craft stick. Drop the letter into the jar and lay the craft stick across the top to hold the letter in place.

Crystals will begin to form on the pipe cleaner in several hours to several days. Once your letter is covered in crystals, remove it from the solution to admire.

Letters in the Salt Tray

Good activity for:

- Promoting sensory-rich play

Materials needed:

- Tray
- Salt
- Optional: Montessori sandpaper letters

Directions:

Add salt to a tray until it just barely covers the entire bottom.

Invite your child to use their index finger to write letters in the tray.

If your child needs help remembering the letter shapes, offer a set of Montessori sandpaper letters for reference.

Shaving Cream Letters

Good activity for:

- Promoting sensory-rich, messy play

Materials needed:

- Tray
- Shaving cream
- Optional: Towels or napkins
- Optional: Montessori sandpaper letters
- Optional: Apron or smock to protect children's clothing

Directions:

Squirt a dollop of shaving cream onto the tray. Encourage your child to spread the shaving cream all over the tray with their hands to make a "writing" surface.

Once the shaving cream is sufficiently spread out, have your child use their index finger to write letters in the shaving cream.

You may wish to have a towel or napkin available for children who want to wipe the shaving cream from their hands.

If your child needs help remembering the letter shapes, offer a set of Montessori sandpaper letters for reference.

Mess-Free Finger Painted Letters

Good activity for:

- Promoting sensory-rich play
- Developing fine motor skills

Materials needed:

- Quart-size zip top plastic bag
- Tempera paint
- Tape
- Optional: Q-tip
- Optional: Montessori sandpaper letters

Directions:

Add just enough tempera paint to a zip top plastic bag to create a thin coat of paint throughout the bag. Use your fingers to spread the paint around.

To prevent a mess, seal the top of the bag shut with tape. You may also want to tape the bag to your child's work surface.

Invite your child to write letters in the paint. Your child can write with their finger or with a Q-tip.

If your child needs help remembering the letter shapes, offer a set of Montessori sandpaper letters for reference.

Space-Themed Writing Tray

Good activity for:

- Supporting sensory-rich play
- Developing fine motor skills
- Engaging children who love outer space

Materials needed:

- Tray (or baking pan)
- Salt
- Blue liquid watercolor paint (or blue food dye)
- Space figurines
- Optional: Montessori sandpaper letters

Directions:

Pour salt into a tray until it barely covers the entire bottom. Add drops of blue liquid watercolor paint or food dye and stir to color the salt. Add a few space figurines to complete the tray.

Tell your child that the sand is "moon dust," and show them how to use their index finger to write letters in the "moon dust."

After writing a letter, your child can give the tray a gentle shake to "erase" the letter.

If your child needs help remembering the letter shapes, offer a set of Montessori sandpaper letters for reference.

"Magic Paint" Letters

Good activity for:

- Taking learning outside
- Combining letter learning and the science of evaporation

Materials needed:

- Bowl of water ("magic paint")
- Paint brush
- Open area of concrete

Directions:

Bring a paint brush and a bowl of water (i.e., "magic paint") outside. Explain to your child that they will be using "magic paint" to write letters on the concrete.

Explain that "magic paint" looks clear, but briefly becomes visible when painted on concrete. But because it is magic, the paint disappears after a little while.

Have your child dip the brush into the "magic paint" and start painting letters on the concrete. On hot days, due to accelerated evaporation, the letters will disappear very quickly.

Glitter Glue Letters

Good activity for:

- Developing fine motor skills
- Engaging children who love using glitter glue

Materials needed:

- Glitter glue
- Cardstock (or paper)
- Optional: Montessori sandpaper letters

Directions:

Provide your child with a bottle of glitter glue. Then name a letter for your child to make.

Have your child draw the letter on cardstock with the glitter glue.

If your child needs help remembering the letter shapes, offer a set of Montessori sandpaper letters for reference.

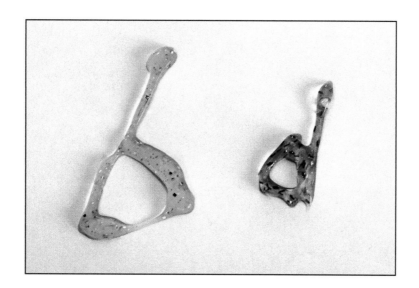

Rainbow Writing

Good activity for:

- Capturing the interest of children who enjoy making rainbows

Materials needed:

- *Letter Outlines* printable (p. 136)
- Red, orange, yellow, green, blue, and purple crayons (or markers)
- Printer
- Printer paper
- Optional: Scissors

Directions:

Print the pages you need from the *Letter Outlines* printable.

Invite your child to make rainbow letters by writing inside the letter outlines with all the colors of the rainbow, first with red, then orange, yellow, green, blue, and purple.

By doing this, your child will practice writing each letter a total of six times while making some pretty rainbow art.

Window Writing

Good activity for:

- Practicing proper pencil grip
- Strengthening shoulders, arms, and hands

Materials needed:

- Wet erase markers
- Window or glass door at child's height
- Damp rag or paper towels for cleaning
- Optional: Montessori sandpaper letters

Directions:

Make sure your child understands that they will be writing on windows with special markers, but that they are not allowed to write on windows or walls at other times.

Encourage your child to write letters on the window. You can draw horizontal lines to keep their writing straight and level if needed.

Show your child how to erase their work with a damp rag or paper towel when done.

If your child needs help remembering the letter shapes, offer a set of Montessori sandpaper letters for reference.

Icy Letter Writing

Good activity for:

- Promoting sensory-rich play
- Engaging children who like the feel of ice

Materials needed:

- Construction paper
- Bowl of ice
- Towel or glove to protect your child's hands while holding the cold ice
- Optional: Montessori sandpaper letters

Directions:

Place a piece of construction paper in front of your child along with a bowl of ice. Invite your child to use the ice to "write" on the paper. Have your child hold the ice with a towel or glove.

As your child writes, liquid water will melt off the ice, wetting the construction paper and causing it to turn a darker color.

If your child needs help remembering the letter shapes, offer a set of Montessori sandpaper letters for reference.

Letter Tic-Tac-Toe

Good activity for:

- Engaging children who enjoy playing tic-tac-toe

Materials needed:

- White board (or paper)
- Dry erase markers (or pencils)
- White board eraser

Directions:

Tic-tac-toe is played with two players. You can play with your child, or two children can play together.

Begin by drawing a 3x3 grid. Tic-tac-toe is usually played using x's and o's, but in this version any letter of the alphabet can be used. Decide ahead of time which letter each player will use to mark their spots.

Players take turns writing letters in the grid. The game ends when one player gets three letters in a row and is designated the winner. Or, if all nine spaces are filled in with no winner, the game is declared a tie.

Letter Writing with a Feather Quill

Good activity for:

- Combining letter learning with a history lesson

Materials needed:

- Feather quill
- Parchment-style paper (or brown construction paper)
- Black ink (or black liquid watercolor paint) in a small container
- Optional: Tray to contain any mess
- Optional: Montessori sandpaper letters

Directions:

Purchase a feather quill or use an online tutorial to make your own. Provide your child with ink and parchment paper (or use brown construction paper as a substitute).

Explain to your child that a very long time ago people used to write with feather quills instead of pens.

Show your child how to dip the feather quill into the ink and use it to write letters on the paper.

If needed, provide your child with Montessori sandpaper letters to refer to.

Sandpaper Writing

Good activity for:

- Exploring new textures
- Engaging children who love the feel of sandpaper

Materials needed:

- Sandpaper
- Crayons
- Optional: Montessori sandpaper letters

Directions:

Provide your child with a sheet of sandpaper and a crayon. Have them use the crayon to write letters on the sandpaper. Don't worry if the letters turn out a bit crooked due to the texture of the sandpaper.

After writing letters, invite your child to use their finger to trace the letters they have written on the sandpaper.

If your child needs help remembering the letter shapes, offer a set of Montessori sandpaper letters for reference.

Geoboard Letters

Good activity for:

- Developing fine motor skills
- Engaging children who enjoy using geoboards

Materials needed:

- Geoboard
- Rubber bands
- Optional: Montessori sandpaper letters

Directions:

Invite your child to make letters on a geoboard using rubber bands.

Call out letters for your child to form, or have them chose their own letters to form.

If needed, provide your child with Montessori sandpaper letters to refer to.

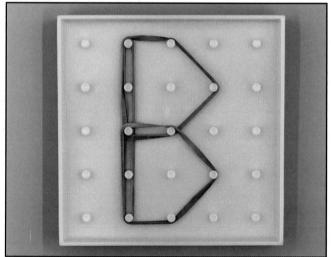

Straw and Pipe Cleaner Letters

Good activity for:

- Developing fine motor skills

Materials needed:

- Straws
- Pipe cleaners
- Child-friendly scissors
- Optional: Montessori sandpaper letters

Directions:

Show your child how to make letters using straws and pipe cleaners.

Use straws to form straight lines and pipe cleaners to form curvy lines. Your child can use pipe cleaners to hold straw sections together.

If your child needs help remembering the letter shapes, offer a set of Montessori sandpaper letters for reference.

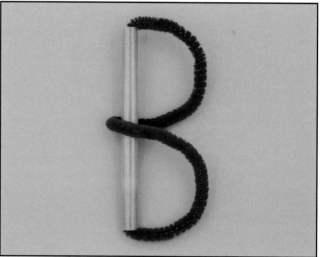

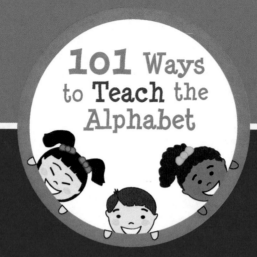

101 Ways to Teach the Alphabet

CHAPTER FIVE

• •

Activities That Teach Letter Case Matching

Planting Letters Case Matching

Good activity for:

- Engaging children in pretend garden play

Materials needed:

- Flower pots
- Craft sticks
- Foam flower stickers
- Permanent marker

Directions:

Write several uppercase letters on foam flowers and stick one each on the side of the flower pots.

Write the corresponding lowercase letters on foam flowers and attach them to the ends of craft sticks.

Have your child "plant" the flowers in pots labeled with the corresponding uppercase letter to make a beautiful flower garden.

Milk Cap Letter Case Matching

Good activity for:

- Developing fine motor skills

Materials needed:

- *Letter Case Matching with Milk Caps* printable (p. 877)
- Milk caps, cleaned and dried
- Optional: Container to hold the milk caps
- Permanent marker
- Printer
- Printer paper or cardstock
- Optional: Laminator

Directions:

Print the worksheets you need from the *Letter Case Matching with Milk Caps* printable. For greater durability, print on cardstock and/or laminate the pages.

Using the letters on the worksheet for reference, use a permanent marker to write letters on the top side of the milk caps. Underline letters that can be easily confused (such as 'd' and 'p').

Have your child place each milk cap with a lowercase letter on top of the corresponding uppercase letter.

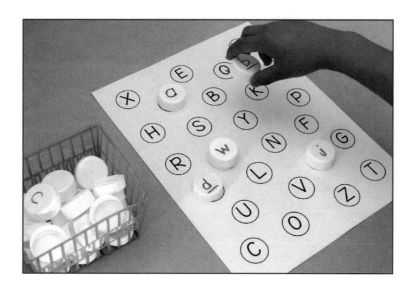

Ice Cream Letter Case Matching

Good activity for:

- Engaging children in ice cream-related pretend play

Materials needed:

- *Ice Cream Letter Case Matching* printable (p. 886)
- Scissors
- Printer
- Printer paper or cardstock
- Optional: Laminator

Directions:

Print the *Ice Cream Letter Case Matching* printable. For greater durability, print on cardstock and/or laminate the pages.

Cut the cone cards and the ice cream cards along the solid lines. Then mix them up.

Have your child make ice cream cones by matching the lowercase letter on the ice cream with the corresponding uppercase letter on the cone.

For added fun, your child can pretend to serve the ice cream for others to "eat."

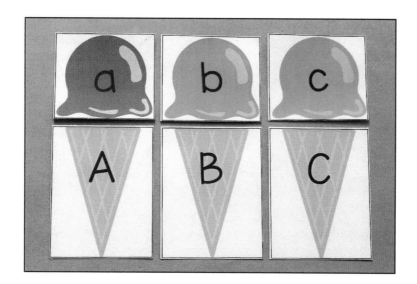

Muffin Tin Letter Case Matching

Good activity for:

- Stimulating creative use of household materials

Materials needed:

- Muffin tin
- Uppercase letter tiles
- Lowercase letter beads

Directions:

Put one uppercase letter tile into each cup of the muffin tin. Place corresponding lowercase letter beads to the side.

Invite your child to match the uppercase and lowercase letters by dropping each lowercase letter bead into the muffin cup with the matching uppercase letter tile.

Letter Case Matching Dominoes

Good activity for:

- Engaging children who enjoy playing dominoes

Materials needed:

- *Letter Case Matching Dominoes* printable (p. 896)
- Scissors
- Printer
- Printer paper or cardstock
- Optional: Laminator

Directions:

Print the domino sets you need from the *Letter Case Matching Dominoes* printable. For greater durability, print on cardstock and/or laminate the pages.

Have your child find the starting domino, marked by a green dot. They should place it on the work surface and identify the uppercase letter on the domino. Then they should find the domino with the corresponding lowercase letter and set it just to the right of the first domino.

Your child should continue placing dominoes until reaching the last domino, marked with a red dot.

Dot Sticker Letter Case Matching

Good activity for:

- Developing fine motor skills
- Engaging children who enjoy playing with stickers

Materials needed:

- *Letter Case Matching with Dot Stickers* printable (p. 906)
- Dot stickers 1 inch (2.5 cm) in diameter
- Marker
- Printer
- Printer paper

Directions:

Print the worksheets you need from the *Letter Case Matching with Dot Stickers* printable.

Using the letters on the worksheet for reference, use a marker to write letters on the dot stickers. Underline letters that can be easily confused (such as 'd' and 'p').

Have your child place the dot sticker letters over the corresponding letters on the worksheet.

Case Matching with Sticky Notes

Good activity for:

- Doing a quick, low-prep case matching activity

Materials needed:

- Sticky notes in two different colors
- Marker

Directions:

On one set of sticky notes, write several uppercase letters. On the other set of sticky notes, write the corresponding lowercase letters. Underline letters that can be easily confused (such as 'd' and 'p').

Scatter the uppercase letters across a wall. Then hand your child the lowercase letters and have them place each one on the wall next to its corresponding uppercase letter.

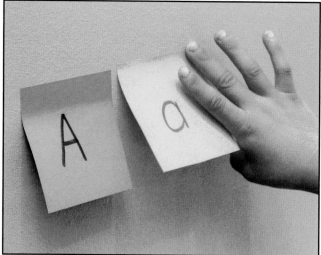

Magazine Letter Hunt and Case Sorting

Good activity for:

- Developing scissor skills
- Practicing sorting skills

Materials needed:

- *Magazine Letter Hunt & Case Sorting* printable (p. 913)
- Child-friendly scissors
- Magazines or catalogues
- Glue stick
- Printer
- Printer paper

Directions:

Print the worksheets you need from the *Magazine Letter Hunt & Case Sorting* printable.

Invite your child to search through magazines or catalogues for the target letter. Have your child cut out the letters and glue them onto their worksheet, sorting them into the appropriate boxes for uppercase and lowercase letters.

Help the Mama Letter Find Her Babies

Good activity for:

- Engaging children who love to play "house"

Materials needed:

- Uppercase Montessori sandpaper letters
- Lowercase letter beads
- Optional: Houses for each letter family

Directions:

If using houses, put the uppercase letters in front of their respective homes. Otherwise, just spread the uppercase letters across the work surface. Then scatter the lowercase letters around.

Tell your child that the uppercase letters are the "mama" letters and the lowercase letters are the "baby" letters. The "mama" letters need help finding their babies.

Have your child move all the "baby" lowercase letters next to their "mama" uppercase letters.

Case Matching Clip Cards

Good activity for:

- Developing fine motor skills
- Providing children with self-correcting learning tasks (control of error)

Materials needed:

- *Letter Case Matching Clip Cards* printable (p. 941)
- Clothespins
- Printer
- Printer paper or cardstock
- Optional: Laminator
- Scissors

Directions:

Print and prepare the *Letter Case Matching Clip Cards* printable according to the directions. For greater durability, print on cardstock and/or laminate the pages.

You may wish to put a small dot on the back of each clip card to indicate which letter is the correct answer so that children can check their work independently.

Give the cards and clothespins to your child. Invite your child to clip the lowercase letter on the right side of the card that corresponds to the uppercase letter on the left side of the card.

Case Matching with String and Tape

Good activity for:

- Promoting active learning

Materials needed:

- Sticky notes
- Marker
- String
- Painter's tape
- Scissors

Directions:

Write uppercase letters and the corresponding lowercase letters on sticky notes. Stick the uppercase and lowercase letters on a wall in separate vertical lines about 2 feet (2/3 meter) apart. Place the uppercase and lowercase letters in different orders (e.g., 'Q,' 'E,' 'G' vs. 'e,' 'g,' 'q').

For each set of letters, cut one piece of string about 3 feet long (1 meter). Cut two small pieces of painter's tape for each piece of string.

Have your child tape one end of each string next to an uppercase letter and the other end next to the matching lowercase letter.

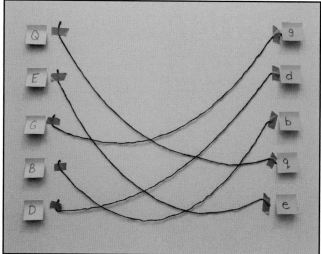

Stamp the Letter

Good activity for:

- Engaging children who enjoy using rubber stamps

Materials needed:

- *Stamp the Letter* printable (p. 949)
- Letter stamps
- Ink pad
- Printer
- Printer paper

Directions:

Print the worksheets you need from the *Stamp the Letter* printable.

Have your child identify each letter on the worksheet.

If the worksheet has uppercase letters, your child should find and stamp the corresponding lowercase letters in the spaces provided. If the worksheet has lowercase letters, your child should find and stamp the corresponding uppercase letters in the spaces provided.

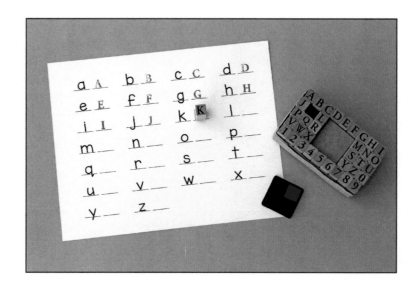

Letter Case Matching Puzzles

Good activity for:

- Providing children with self-correcting learning tasks (control of error)

Materials needed:

- *Letter Case Matching Puzzles* printable (p. 954)
- Scissors
- Printer
- Printer paper or cardstock
- Optional: Laminator

Directions:

Print and prepare the letter puzzles you need from the *Letter Case Matching Puzzles* printable according to the printable directions. For greater durability, print on cardstock and/or laminate the pages.

Have your child assemble the puzzles by matching the uppercase and lowercase letters.

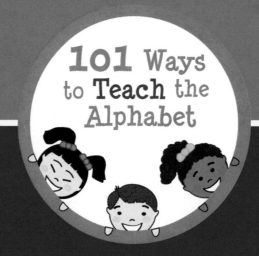

101 Ways
to **Teach** the
Alphabet

CHAPTER SIX

● ● ● ● ● ● ● ● ● ● ● ● ● ● ● ● ● ● ● ●

Reference
Resources

Sample Letter Sequences

In general, teaching lowercase letters first supports an earlier transition into reading (because most print is lowercase), while teaching uppercase letters first supports early writing attempts (because uppercase letters are generally easier to write).

These first three letter sequences focus on teaching high-utility lowercase letters early on so children can quickly begin sounding out words like *at*, *in*, *sat*, *cat*, *rip*, *pin*, and *tap*.

Sequence #1: **s m a t** • **c r i p** • **b f o g** • **h j u l** • **d w e n** • **k q v x y z**

Sequence #2: **s m t a p f c** • **r b l i g n d** • **h j k w o u v** • **y z x q e**

Sequence #3: **s a t i p n** • **c k e h r** • **m d g o** • **l f b q u** • **j z w** • **v y x**

This next sequence focuses on teaching uppercase letters that are easy to write before uppercase letters that are more difficult to write.

Sequence #4: **L E F H T I V X W N Y M K A Z C O G Q B D J P U R S**

This next sequence focuses on teaching uppercase letters in a way that minimizes letter reversals while promoting good stroke habits.

Sequence #5: **F E D P B R N M** • **H K L U V W X Y A** • **C O Q G S A I T J**

This next sequence teaches lowercase letters based on how easy they are to write.

Sequence #6: **l t i v w x o z k y h r n m c e f j u a b p d g q s**

Letter Pairs to Introduce Separately

Lowercase Letter Pairs

Here is a list of lowercase letter pairs that should be introduced separately:

- a-o
- b-d
- b-h
- b-p
- c-e
- c-k
- c-o
- d-f
- f-t
- f-v
- g-k
- g-p
- g-q
- h-n
- i-j
- i-l
- m-n
- m-w
- n-u
- p-q
- s-z
- u-v
- v-w
- v-y

Uppercase Letter Pairs

Here is a list of uppercase letter pairs that should be introduced separately:

- B-D
- C-G
- C-K
- D-F
- D-O
- D-T
- E-F
- F-V
- I-L
- K-X
- M-N
- M-W
- O-Q
- P-R
- S-Z
- U-V
- V-Y

Short and Long Vowel Sounds

Short vowel sounds

A says /ă/ as in apple or pat

E says /ĕ/ as in egg or ten

I says /ĭ/ as in igloo or pig

O says /ŏ/ as in otter or sock

U says /ŭ/ as in umbrella or mud

Long vowel sounds

A says /ā/ as in apron or cake

E says /ē/ as in eagle or feet

I says /ī/ as in ice or bike

O says /ō/ as in open or hope

U says /ū/ as in unicorn or cube

Pencil Grip Development

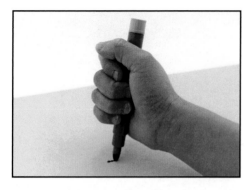

Stage 1: Fisted or palmar supinate grip

Children ages 1 to 2 typically hold the pencil like a dagger with their fist closed around it. In this grip, all five fingers hold the pencil. Pencil movement at this stage usually comes from the shoulder rather than the arm, wrist, or fingers.

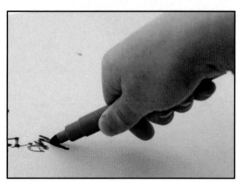

Stage 2: Radial cross palmar grip

Children ages 2 to 3 begin to hold the pencil with more support from the thumb and fingers. With this grip, the thumb is close to the tip of the pencil. Pencil movement at this stage comes from the arm with some support from the shoulder.

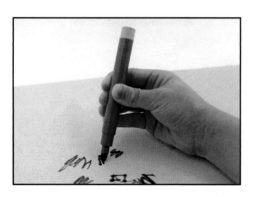

Stage 3: Five-finger or modified tripod grip

Children ages 3 to 5 begin to hold the pencil with all five fingers. Pencil movement at this stage comes primarily from the wrist.

Stage 4: Three-finger or tripod grasp

Children ages 4 to 6 begin to use the mature three-finger grip where the thumb and first finger pinch the pencil and the third finger provides support. The fourth and fifth fingers get tucked out of the way. Pencil movement at this stage comes from the fingers.

Chapter 7 features 800+ pages
of printable alphabet materials for use
with the activities in this book.

Download Chapter 7 at:

www.giftofcuriosity.com/chapter7/

Made in the USA
Coppell, TX
07 August 2021